T0268879

Treasures from the Spiritual Classics

ABBA
by
EVELYN UNDERHILL

Compiled by
Roger L. Roberts

Morehouse Publishing
NEW YORK · HARRISBURG · DENVER

First USA Edition published 1982
Morehouse Publishing,
4775 Linglestown Road, Harrisburg, PA 17112
445 Fifth Avenue, New York, NY 10016

Morehouse Publishing is an imprint of Church Publishing Incorporated.

PREFACE

MOST CHRISTIAN people often find it difficult to say their prayers in any meaningful way. Here, in these extracts from a book of devotional meditations by Evelyn Underhill, will be found clear but profound guidance on how to pray.

The title of the book, *Abba*, is the term used in more than one place in the New Testament for addressing God as Father and it is with the 'Our Father' prayer that these meditations are concerned. At first sight it might be thought impossible to say anything fresh on something so familiar to all Christians as the Lord's Prayer. Yet the inexhaustible depths of meaning to be found in it may, by the very fact of familiarity, all too easily escape notice and understanding.

In these meditations those depths are explored with passionate intensity by an acknowledged expert in Christian mysticism. Both as a scholar of widely recognised academic distinction in her chosen field of study and as one of the leading conductors of Retreats in her day, Evelyn Underhill (1875—1941) proved to have an unusual gift for combining spiritual perception of a rare order and a deep sympathy with the human situation. These qualities are well illustrated in the eloquent work from which these extracts have been taken. They will be found to illuminate brilliantly the dark places encountered by the soul in its approach through prayer to the Majesty and Mystery of Almighty God.

R.L.R.

The extracts which follow are reprinted with permission from Evelyn Underhill's *Abba*, first published in 1940 by Longmans, Green & Co Ltd.

HOW TO PRAY

THE NEW TESTAMENT has preserved for us, in our Lord's reply to His followers, a complete description of what Christian prayer should be; its character and objective; its balance and proportion; its quality and tone. As we explore this description and try to realize all that is implied in it, we find the whole world of prayer, its immense demands and immense possibilities, opening before us. Yet in accordance with that steady hold on history, that deep respect for the tradition within which He appeared, which marks the whole of Christ's teaching, the description was given—as the answer to those who asked for the secret of Eternal Life was given—in words which were already familiar to the askers: in seven linked phrases which were a part of Jewish prayer, and can be traced to their origin in the Old Testament. It is as if we went to a saint and asked him to teach us to pray, and he replied by reciting the Quinquagesima

7

Collect. We can imagine the disappointment of the disciples—'We knew all this before!' The answer to this objection is the same as the answer to the Lawyer: this *do* and you shall live. You already have all the information. Invest it with realism, translate it into action: phrases into facts, theology into religion. I am not giving you a set formula for repetition, but several complementary pictures of the one life of prayer.

It is too often supposed that when our Lord said, 'In this manner pray ye.' He meant not 'these are the right dispositions and longings, the fundamental acts of every soul that prays,' but 'this is the form of words which, above all others, Christians are required to repeat.' As a consequence this is the prayer in which, with an almost incredible stupidity, they have found the material of those vain repetitions which He has specially condemned. Again and again in public and private devotion the Lord's Prayer is taken on hurried lips, and recited at a pace which makes impossible any

8

realization of its tremendous claims and profound demands. Far better than this cheapening of the awful power of prayer was the practice of the old woman described by St. Teresa, who spent an hour over the first two words, absorbed in reverence and love.

It is true, of course, that this pattern in its verbal form, its obvious and surface meaning, is far too familiar to us. Rapid and frequent repetition has reduced it to a formula. We are no longer conscious of its mysterious beauty and easily assume that we have long ago exhausted its inexhaustible significance. The result of this persistent error has been to limit our understanding of the great linked truths which are here given to us; to harden their edges, and turn an instruction which sets up a standard for each of the seven elements of prayer, and was intended to govern our whole life towards God, into a set form of universal obligation.

This is a sovereign instance of that spiritual stupidity with which we treat the 'awful and mysterious truths' religion reveals to us; truths of which Coleridge has rightly said, that they are commonly 'considered so true as to lose all the powers of truth, and lie bedridden in the dormitory of the soul.'[1] But when we 'centre down,' as Quakers say, from the surface of human life to its deeps, and rouse those sleeping truths and take them with us, and ask what they look like there—in the secret place where the soul is alone with God and knows its need of God—then, all looks different. These great declarations disclose their intensity of life, their absolute quality; as a work of art which has hung respected and unloved in a public gallery glows with new meaning when we bring it into the home or the sanctuary for which it was really made. Seen thus, the Paternoster reminds us how rich and various, how deeply rooted in the Supernatural, the Christian life is or should be, moving from awestruck worship to

[1]Coleridge's *Table Talk*, 28th June, 1834.

homely confidence, and yet one: how utterly it depends on God, yet how searching is the demand it makes on man. 'Every just man,' says Osuna, 'needs the seven things for which this prayer—or this scheme of prayer—asks.'[2] Taken together they cover all the realities of our situation, at once beset by nature and cherished by grace: establishing Christian prayer as a relation between wholes, between man in his completeness and God who is all.

And we note their order and proportion. First, four clauses entirely concerned with our relation to God; then three concerned with our human situation and needs. Four hinge on the First Commandment, three hinge on the Second. Man's twisted, thwarted and embittered nature, his state of sin, his sufferings, helplessness, and need, do not stand in the foreground; but the splendour and beauty of God, demanding a self-oblivion so complete that it transforms suffering, and blots out even

[2]*The Third Spiritual Alphabet.* Treatise 13.

II

the memory of sin. We begin with a sublime yet intimate invocation of Reality, which plunges us at once into the very ground of the Universe and claims kinship with the enfolding mystery. Abba, Father. The Infinite God is the Father of my soul. We end by the abject confession of our dependence and need of guidance: of a rescue and support coming to our help right down in the jungle of life. Following the path of the Word Incarnate, this prayer begins on the summits of spiritual experience and comes steadily down from the Infinite to the finite, from the Spaceless to the little space on which we stand. Here we find all the strange mixed experience of man, over-ruled by the unchanging glory and charity of God.

CHILDREN OF THE FATHER

The crowds who followed Christ hoping for healing or counsel did not ask Him to teach them how to pray; nor did He give this prayer to them. It is not for those who want religion to be helpful, who seek after signs; those who expect it to solve their political problems and cure their diseases, but are not prepared to share its cost. He gave it to those whom He was going to incorporate into His rescuing system, use in His ministry; the sons of the Kingdom, self-given to the creative purposes of God. '*Thou* when thou prayest . . . pray ye on this manner.' It is the prayer of those 'sent forth' to declare the Kingdom, whom the world will hate, whose unpopularity with man will be in proportion to their loyalty to God; the apostles of the Perfect in whom, if they are true to their vocation, the Spirit of the Father will speak. The disciples sent out to do Christ's work were to depend on prayer, an unbroken communion with the Eternal; and this is the sort of prayer on which they were to depend. We therefore, when we dare to use it, offer ourselves by implication as their fellow workers for the Kingdom; for it supposes and requires an unconditional and

13

filial devotion to the interests of God. Those who use the prayer must pray from the Cross.

Men have three wants, which only God can satisfy. They need food, for they are weak and dependent. They need forgiveness, for they are sinful. They need guidance, for they are puzzled. Give—Forgive—Lead—Deliver. All their prayer can be reduced to the loving adoration of the Father and the confident demand for His help.

'Our Father, which art in heaven.' We are the children of God and therefore inheritors of heaven. Here is the source alike of our hope and our penitence; the standard which confounds us, the essence of religion, the whole of prayer. 'Heaven is God and God is my soul,' says Elisabeth de la Trinité. It is a statement of fact, which takes us clean away from the world of religious problems and consolations, the world of self-interested worries and strivings, and discloses the infinite span and unfathomable depth of that supernatural world in which we really live. From our distorted life 'unquieted with dreads, bounden with cares, busied with vanities, vexed with temptations'[1] the soul in its prayer reaches out to centre its trust on the Eternal, the existent.

In those rare glimpses of Christ's own life of prayer which the Gospels vouchsafe to us, we always notice the perpetual reference to the unseen Father; so much more vividly present to Him than anything that is seen. Behind that daily life into which He entered so generously, filled as it was with constant appeals to His practical pity and help, there is ever the sense of that strong and tranquil Presence, ordering all things and bringing them to their appointed end; not with a rigid and mechanical precision, but with the freedom of a living, creative, cherishing thought and love. Throughout His life, the secret, utterly obedient conversation of Jesus with His Father goes on. He always snatches opportunities for it,

[1] *The Imitation of Christ.* Bk. III, cap. 48.

15

and at every crisis He returns to it as the unique source of confidence and strength; the right and reasonable relation between the soul and its Source.

I thank thee, Heavenly Father, because thou hast hidden these things from the wise and prudent and revealed them unto babes . . . Even so, Father, for so it seemed good in thy sight. . . . I have kept my Father's commandment and abide in his love . . . Father, the hour is come. . . . O righteous Father! the world knew thee not, but I knew thee. . . . Father, if thou be willing, remove this cup from me. . . . Father, forgive them . . . into thy hands I commend my spirit.

Though our human experience of God cannot maintain itself on such a level as this, yet for us too as members of Christ these words have significance. They set the standard of realism, of childlike and confident trust which must govern our relation to the Unseen.

Abba: Evelyn Underhill

Abba, Father. The personalist note, never absent from a fully operative religion, is struck at the start; and all else that is declared or asked is brought within the aura of this relationship. Our sins, aims, struggles, sufferings, our easy capitulation to hopelessness and fear, look different over against that truth. Our responsibilities become simplified, and are seen to be one single, filial responsibility to God. Our Father, which art in heaven, yet present here and now in and with our struggling lives; on whom we depend utterly, as children of the Eternal Perfect whose nature and whose name is Love.

'Ye are of God, little children.' Were this our realistic belief and the constant attitude of our spirits, our whole life, inward and outward, would be transformed. For we are addressing One who is already there, already in charge of the situation, and knowing far more about that situation than we do ourselves. Within His span it already lies complete, from its origin to its end. 'Your Father knoweth what things ye have need of before you ask him.' The prevenience of God is the dominant fact of all life; and therefore of the life of prayer. We, hard and loveless, already stand in heaven. We open the stiff doors of our hearts and direct our fluctuating wills to a completely present Love and Will directing, moulding and creating us.

And moreover in these first words, the praying soul accepts once for all its true status as a member of the whole family of man. Our Father. It can never again enter into prayer as a ring-fenced individual, intent on a private relation with God; for this is a violation of the law of Charity. Its prayer must overflow the boundaries of selfhood to include the life, the needs of the race; accepting as a corollary of its filial relation with God a brotherly relation with all other souls however diverse, and at every point replacing 'mine' by 'ours'. This wide spreading love, this refusal of private advantage is the very condition of Christian prayer; for that prayer is an instrument of redemptive action, not merely of personal achievement.

Here my enemy prays by my side, since the world of prayer has no frontiers; and in so doing he ceases to be my enemy, because we meet in God.

THE HOLY NAME

Hallowed be Thy Name. The modern mind, living sometimes prudently and sometimes carelessly, but never theocentrically, cannot make anything of such words as these; for they sweep the soul up, past the successive and the phenomenal, and leave it in abject adoration before the single reality of God.

This first response of creation to its author, this awestruck hallowing of the Name, must also be the first response of the praying soul. If we ask how this shall be done within the individual life and what it will require of us in obligation and adjustment, perhaps the answer will be something like this: 'Our Father,

which art in heaven, hallowed, revered, be
Thy mysterious Name in my dim and fluctuating soul, to which Thou hast revealed
Thyself in such a degree as I can endure. May
all my contacts and relationships, my struggles and temptations, thoughts, dreams and
desires be coloured by this loving reverence.
Let me ever look through and beyond circum-
stance to Thee, so that all I am and do may
become more and more worthy of the God
who is the origin of all. Let me never take
such words on my lips that I could not pass
from them to the hallowing of Thy Name.
(That one principle alone, consistently applied, would bring order and charity into the
centre of my life.) May that Name, too, be
hallowed in my work, keeping me in re-
membrance that Thou art the doer of all that
is really done: my part is that of a humble
collaborator, giving of my best.' This means
that adoration, a delighted recognition of the
life and action of God, subordinating everything to the Presence of the Holy, is the es-

sential preparation for action. That stops all feverish strain, all rebellion and despondency, all sense of our own importance, all worry about our own success; and so gives dignity, detachment, tranquillity to our action and may make it of some use to Him.

Thus the four words of this petition can cover, criticize and re-interpret the whole of our personal life; cleansing it from egoism, orientating it towards reality, and reminding us that our life and work are without significance, except in so far as they glorify that God to whom nothing is adequate though everything is dear. Our response to each experience which He puts in our path, for the greatest disclosure of beauty to the smallest appeal to love, from perfect happiness to utmost grief, will either hallow or not hallow His Name; and this is the only thing that matters about it. For every call to admiration or to sacrifice is an intimation of the Holy, the Other; and opens a path leading out from self to God. These words, then, form in themselves a complete prayer; an aspiration which includes every level and aspect of life. It is the sort of prayer that both feeds and expresses the life of a saint, in its absolute disinterestedness and delighted abasement before the Perfection of God.

From one point of view the rest of the Lord's Prayer is simply about the different ways in which this adoring response of creation can be made more complete; for it asks for the sanctification of the universe. And by universe we do not mean some vast abstraction. We mean everything that exists, visible and invisible; the small as well as the great, the hosts of earth as well as the hosts of heaven; the mouse's tail as well as the seraph's wing brought into the circle of holiness and transfigured by the radiance of God. All creatures without exception taking part in the one great utterance of the Name: all self-interested striving transformed into that one great striving for the Glory of God which is the whole life of Heaven and should be the whole life of earth.

If the transforming power of religion is to be felt, its discipline must be accepted, its price paid in every department of life; and it is only when the soul is awakened to the reality and call of God, known at every point of its multiple experience, that it is willing to pay the price and accept the discipline. Worship is a primary means of this awakening.

It follows once more that whole-hearted adoration is the only real preparation for right action: action which develops within the Divine atmosphere, and is in harmony with the eternal purposes of God. The Bible is full of illustrations of this truth, from the call of Isaiah to the Annunciation. First the awestruck recognition of God: and then, the doing of His Will. We cannot discern His Eternal Purpose, even as it affects our tiny lives, opportunities and choices, except with the eyes of disinterested and worshipping love. The hallowing of the Name is therefore the essen-

23

tial condition without which it is not possible to work for the Kingdom or recognize the pressure of the Will. So the first imperative of the life of prayer is that which the humanist finds so hard to understand. We are to turn our backs upon earth, and learn how to deal with its sins and its needs by looking steadfastly up to heaven.

Yet the life of prayer is incomplete if it stops here, in the realm of aspiration. Costly action as well as delighted fervour must form part of it. Like all else in the spiritual life of animal man, it must have its sacramental expression. Heroic sacrifice, peaceful suffering, patient and inconspicuous devotion to uncongenial tasks, the steady fight against sin, ugliness, squalor, and disease, the cleansing of national thought and increase of brotherhood among men: all this is our response to the impact of Perfection, our active recognition of the claim of God. Awe alone is sterile. But when it is married to sacrificial love, the fruits of the Spirit begin to appear; and the hallowing of the Name and the working for the Kingdom are seen to be two sides of one reality—the response of the creature to the demand of Love.

THE COMING OF THE KINGDOM

Having recognized and worshipped the Name, we pray next for its triumph: Thy Kingdom come. Here man's most sacred birthright, his deep longing for perfection, and with it his bitter consciousness of imperfection, break out with power. We want to bring the God whom we worship, His beauty, His sovereignty, His order, into the very texture of our life; and the fundamental human need for action into the radius of our prayer. This is the natural sequel to the prayer of adoration. We have had a glimpse of the mystery of the Holy, have worshipped before the veils of beauty and sacrifice; and that throws into vivid relief the poverty, the anarchy, the unreality in which we live—the resistance of the world, the creature to God, and its awful need of God.

Thy Kingdom come! We open our gates to the Perfect, and entreat its transfiguring presence; redeeming our poor contingencies, our disharmonies, making good our perpetual fallings short. We face the awful contrast between the Actual and the Real, and acknowledge our need of deliverance from sin; especially that sin of the world, that rebellion of creation against the Holy, which has thrust us out of heaven. The Kingdom is the serenity of God already enfolding us, and seeking to penetrate and redeem the whole of this created order; 'shattering the horror of perpetual night' by a ray of heavenly brightness. We pray for this transformation of life, this healing of its misery and violence, its confusion and unrest, through the coming of the Holy God whom we adore; carrying through to regions still unconquered the great, the primary petition for the hallowing of His Name. That the Splendour over against us may enter,

cleanse and sanctify every level of our existence; give it a new quality, coherence and
meaning.

The prayer is not that we may come into
the Kingdom, for this we cannot do in our
own strength. It is that the Kingdom, the
Wholly Other, may come to us, and become
operative within our order; one thing working
in another, as leaven in our dough, as seed in
our field. We are not encouraged to hope that
the social order will go on evolving from
within, until at last altruism triumphs and
greed is dethroned: nor indeed does history
support this view. So far is this amiable programme from the desperate realities of our
situation, so unlikely is it that human nature
will ever do the work of grace, that now we
entreat the Divine Power to enter history by
His Spirit and by His saints; to redeem,
cleanse, fertilize and rule.

What we look for then is not Utopia, but
something which is given from beyond: Em-
manuel, God with us, the whole creation won

from rebellion and consecrated to the creative purposes of Christ. This means something far more drastic than the triumph of international justice and good social conditions. It means the transfiguration of the natural order by the supernatural: by the Eternal Charity. Though we achieve social justice, liberty, peace itself, though we give our bodies to be burned for these admirable causes, if we lack this we are nothing. For the Kingdom is the Holy not the moral; the Beautiful not the correct; the Perfect not the adequate; Charity not law.

Thus more and more we must expect our small action to be overruled and swallowed up in the vast Divine action; and be ready to offer it, whatever it may be, for the fulfilment of God's purpose, however much this may differ from our purpose. The Christian turns again and again from that bewildered contemplation of history in which God is so easily lost, to the prayer of filial trust in which He is always found; knowing here that those very things which seem to turn to man's disadvantage, may yet work to the Divine advantage. On the frontier between prayer and history stands the Cross, a perpetual reminder of the price by which the Kingdom is brought in. Seen from the world's side it is foolishness; seen from the land of contemplation, it is the Wisdom of God. We live in illusion till that wisdom has touched us; and this touch is the first coming of the Kingdom to the individual soul.

None can guess beforehand with what anguish, what tearing of old hard tissues and habits, the Kingdom will force a path into the soul, and confront self-love in its last fortress with the penetrating demand of God. Yet we cannot use the words, unless we are prepared to pay this price: nor is the prayer of adoration real, unless it leads on to this. When we said, 'Hallowed be Thy Name!' we acknowledged the priority of Holiness. Now we offer ourselves for the purposes of Holiness: handing ourselves over to God that His purposes, great or small, declared or secret, natural or spiritual, may be fulfilled through us and in us, and all that is hostile to His Kingdom done away.

To look with real desire for the coming of the Kingdom means crossing over to God's side; dedicating our powers, whatever they may be, to the triumph of His purpose. The Bible is full of a stern insistence on that action which is ever the corollary of true contemplation. It is here that the praying spirit accepts its most sacred privilege: active and costly co-operation with God—first in respect of its own purification, and then in respect of His creative and redeeming action upon life. Our attitude here must be wide open towards God, exhibiting quite simply our poverty and impurity, acknowledging our second-rateness, but still offering ourselves such as we are. Thy Kingdom come! Here am I, send me. Not the nature-lover's admiration but the labourer's hard work turns the corn-field into the harvest-field. Hard work, which soon loses the aura of romantic devotion; and must be continued through drudgery and exhaustion to the end.

THY WILL BE DONE

We have come down in the course of our prayer from the Infinite to the Finite, from the splendour of God, His present yet unseizable loveliness, to our distracted world; which is meant to be part of that splendour, to radiate that loveliness. Here is the scene in which His will to perfection must be worked out through us, by us, in spite of us. 'Thy will be done in earth, as it is in heaven.' We do not know what possibilities, what mysteries, may still be hidden in the unexpressed design. Yet because each step of this descending prayer is a movement of faith, obedience and love, we bring the Infinite with us; as did Christ Himself when he came down from His nights of communion on the mountain to His redemptive work among men. Here, again,

the life of prayer follows the path of the Incarnation. The Wisdom that came forth from
the mouth of the Most High entered deeply
into the common life, and there accomplished
His transforming and redeeming work. We
too are not to experience eternity and take
up our obligations in respect of it in some
exalted other-worldly region; but here and
now, right down in that common life which
is also dear to God, finding in our homely
experience the raw material of sacrifice, turning its humble duties and relationships into
prayer. Be it unto me according to Thy
Word—here, where I am. Not my will but
Thine be done. This is the act of obligation
which puts life without condition at God's
disposal; and so transforms and sacramental-
izes our experience, and brings the Kingdom
in.

Here we arrive at a prayer of pure realism,
which is also the prayer of confident love: for
what the Will may be, and what it may entail
for us, we do not know. The enthusiastic

forward look towards the coming of the Kingdom, the triumph of the Perfect, is easy; less
easy, the acceptance of those conditions
through and in which it must enter and dominate the lives of men. But if adoration has
indeed done its disentangling work, no hesi-
tations will mar this simple movement of
abandonment. Thy Will: I accept the rule of
God, whatever it may be, for myself, as well
as working for it—the prayer of docility. That
means a total capitulation to the mysterious
Divine purpose; war declared on individual
and corporate self-centredness, death to an
earthbound, meticulous or utilitarian piety. It
asks of the soul a heroic and liberating dedi-
cation to the interests of Reality; that, transcending the problems and needs of our
successive existence, we may be made partners
in the one august enterprise of the Spirit. This,
says St. Paul, is the very meaning of the Passion: 'that they which live shall no longer live
unto themselves . . . wherefore, if any man

33

is in Christ, he is a new creature'[1]—his interests have become identical with those of the supernatural world. 'Our wills are ours to make them thine' is not a mere bit of Victorian moralizing, but an almost perfect description of man's metaphysical state. We ask for our own subordination to Reality, the neutralizing of the rebel will, the deep grace of abandonment. For only 'in Christ,' are the Absolute Will and the will of the creature plaited together, to make the single cord of love.

We all have a preconceived idea of the path which we are to follow, the way in which we shall use our talents best. But in the world of prayer, our eyes cleansed by adoration, we perceive and acknowledge that the initiative lies with God; and only with us in so far as we give our energy to Him and take up our inheritance as Children of God, recognising and welcoming His quiet directive action, His

[1]2 Cor. V, 15, 17.

34

steady pressure within life as the only thing that really matters about it. Nor is this recognition possible to any but those whose surrender is complete. 'There is no more certain way of going wrong,' says Grou, 'than to take for the Will of God all which comes into our hearts or passes through our minds.'[1] This means death to self-will however cunningly disguised; the work that we love done with zest and care, but done God's way not ours, at His pace not ours, for His glory not ours, and laid down without reluctance, as the movement of the Will demands. Also the drudgery that we do not love done too, because that is His will and not ours. Going into business with the single talent which we would prefer to keep clean and unsullied by the rough and tumble of life. Substituting the discipline of the workshop for the free-lance activities of the gifted amateur. Taking on the job that needs doing, the machine that needs

[1] J. N. Grou: *Manuel des Ames Intérieures. De L'Obéissance.*

35

tending, and tending it in the right way, even though it gives little scope to our particular gifts; or accepting the situation quietly, when the job which we seemed to be doing rather well is taken away. 'Thy Will be done' means always being ready for God's sudden No over against our eager and well-meaning Yes: His overruling of our well-considered plans for the increase of His Glory and advancement of His Kingdom, confronting us with His Cross—and usually an unimpressive Cross— at the least appropriate time. All self-willed choices and obstinacy, all feverish intensity drawn out of the work which we supposed to be work for Him; so that it becomes more and more His work in us.

Thus the Christian, if he is to find room for the completing opposites of his illogical experience, is obliged on one hand to say, 'Thy Will be done on, in and through this world with which Thou art present; which is by declaration the object of thy care and the garment of thy praise. Here I accept in sim-

plicity the mysterious drama of creation and
destruction, and with that my own contri-
bution to the great purpose which I cannot
discern. And yet too, Thy Will be done by
me at all costs here and now, over against this
rebel world which so decisively rejects it.'
Christian life and prayer must accept this
paradox, moving to and fro between abandonment and effort; for whatever we affirm
in this sphere must at once be qualified by its
opposite. 'I have learned,' said Nicolas of
Cusa, 'that the place wherein Thou art found
unveiled is girt round with the coincidence of
contradictories.'

DAILY BREAD

In the first part of the Lord's Prayer, we are
wholly concerned with God's glory. We pray
with angelic spirits; creatures whose purposes
are completely harmonized with the Creative
Will. In the second part, we turn from the
Eternal Splendour to our earthly limitations,

and bring before God the burden, neediness and sinfulness of our state. Give us this day our daily bread. With this proclamation of our utter dependence, the presentation before God of the simplest and most fundamental of our needs, we pass from adoration to petition, and enter into the full paradox of Christian prayer: the unspeakable majesty and abiding perfection of the Infinite, and because of that majesty and that perfection, the importance of the claim of the fugitive, the imperfect, the finite.

The Heavens declare the Glory of God . . .
Lord, I call upon thee, haste thee unto me!

There is a natural tendency in man to reverse this order of approach; to come before God in a spirit of heaviness, greatly concerned with his own imperfections, needs and desires—'my soul and its shortcomings,' 'the world and its wants'—and defer the putting on of the garment of praise: that wedding-garment which introduces us into the com-

pany of the sons of God and is the only possible beginning of real prayer. Here, Christ's
teaching and practice are decisive. First the
heavenly, then the earthly. First ascend in
heart and mind to the Eternal, adore the
Father, seek the Kingdom, accept the Will:
and all the rest shall be added unto you. Again
and again the New Testament insists on that.
The contrast of the two worlds is absolute;
but their interpenetration is complete. No human need, however homely, is negligible;
none lies outside the glow of God. There is
no point however tiny on which the whole
power of the Eternal Love does not play. Yet
all the importance of the natural, the deep
pathos of its need and imperfection, abides in
its relation to God the Perfect and its dependence on Him; all its reality in the extent to
which it expresses His Will. 'Adam sinned
when he fell from contemplation,' because in
that moment he lost the clue to the meaning
of life. God is the First and the Last. We shall
never grasp the meaning of our experience,

see it in proportion, unless we begin by seeking His Face.

So now from the august vision of the supernatural order declaring His holiness, and the
living Will which moulds, supports and pene-
trates His creation, 'mightily and sweetly ordering all things,' we turn, awed yet
encouraged, to our little changing world; the
homely arena within which the soul is required to glorify God. That changing world,
too, is completely dependent on Him; incap-
able of embodying His will and beauty, unless
fed, cleansed and guided by the other-wordly
Love. The second part of the Lord's Prayer,
then, taking our situation as it is, brings before God the humbling realities of that natural
life within which He finds us and calls us to
the supernatural life, each in our own way
and degree.

As, in the soul's life, will and grace rise and
fall together, so in its prayer effort and abandonment are not alternatives, but completing
opposites; and without their rightful balance

there is no spiritual health. 'If any will not work, neither shall he eat,' said St. Paul; a precept of spiritual as well as practical application. 'He gave them angels' food from Heaven;' but they had to go out and gather the manna daily for themselves. The discipline of God is bracing; He gives the soul's food and gives it in abundance, but under conditions which make a wholesome demand on us. None are dispensed from taking trouble.

'Give us this day for bread the Word of God from Heaven,' says a version of the Lord's Prayer found in the ancient Irish Gospels. Here man in his ignorance and fragility utters the one and all-sufficing prayer. For he is not fed by bread alone, not even by the appointed Bread of sacramental grace, but 'by every word that proceeds from the Mouth of God'—all the utterances of the Spirit, all the messages given to him by and through life, and which make up life's significance. In all these, bitter or sweet, tasteless and dry or full of savour, God the Father of Spirits feeds our weak and childish spirits; that they may grow and even more feed on Him. *Cresce et manducabis me.*

God gives Himself mainly along two channels: through the soul's daily life and circumstances and through its prayer. In both that soul must always be ready for Him; wide open to receive Him, and willing to accept and absorb without fastidiousness that which is given, however distasteful and unsuitable it may seem. For the Food of Eternal Life is mostly plain bread; and though it has indeed all sweetness and all savour for those who accept it with meekness and love, there is nothing in it to attract a more fanciful religious taste. All life's vicissitudes, each grief, trial or sacrifice, each painful step in self-knowledge, every opportunity of love or renunciation and every humiliating fall, have their place here. All give, in their various ways and disguises, the heavenly Food. A sturdy realism is the mark of this divine self-imparting, and the enabling grace of those who receive.

Throughout His ministry, our Lord emphasized the idea of feeding as something intimately connected with His love and care for souls. The mystery of the Eucharist does not stand alone. It is the crest of a great wave; a total sacramental disclosure of the dealings of the Transcendent God with men. The hunger of man is the matter of Christ's first temptation. The feedings of the four thousand and the five thousand are more than miracles of practical compassion; we feel that in them something of deep significance is done, one of the mysteries of Eternal Life a little bit unveiled. So too in the Supper at Emmaus, when the bread is broken the Holy One is known. It is peculiar to Christianity, indeed part of the mystery of the Incarnation, that it constantly shows us this coming of God through and in homely and fugitive things and events; and puts the need and dependence of the creature at the very heart of prayer.

OUR TRESPASSES

Forgive us our trespasses—our voluntary share in the world's sinfulness—as we forgive them that trespass against us. Penitence is ever the fruit of adoring vision. 'The more holy I find God,' said von Hugel, 'the more wicked I feel myself to be.' 'Thou the Holy, Thou the Strong.' I, the unholy, feeble, sinful; yet able in my weakness to perceive Beauty and adore.

Once again the soul is brought to a closer, more personal apprehension of its true situation; is thrown yet more deeply into God. If we cannot live without His Life feeding and supporting us, still less can we live without His loving-kindness; tolerating our imperfections, rectifying our errors, forgiving our imperfections, rectifying our errors, forgiving our perpetual shortcomings and excesses, debts and trespasses, and giving us again and again another chance. His challenge stands over against us, in its eternal beauty and per-

44

fection: but we know that the standard of eternal perfection must not be applied to us. The adoring soul which worshipped with the seraphim and said, 'Hallowed be Thy Name' now stands by the side of 'Isaiah and shares his creaturely shame. 'Woe is me! for I am a man of unclean lips.' We belong to an imperfect world. That downward pull, that declension from the light, which theology calls original sin, is felt at every level of our being. With the deepening of our experience we become more and more conscious of this. Hence the life of prayer is always a progress in lowliness; and now we arrive at the genuine and life-giving humility which is the fruit of seeing ourselves as we really are. 'Glory be to thee! have mercy upon me!' We take our lowly place, acknowledge our wretchedness; and on this povery and helplessness we base our confident prayer for the indulgent gentleness of God.

Moreover, the scene in which we are placed makes its own drastic demand on prudence and courage. As de Tourville says, it is useless for the Christian to look for a main road on which he can walk safely and steadily to his journey's end. Like the Swiss, he must learn that rough tracks are the native roads of his country; that we only become sure-footed by long practice, and that slips and falls are sure to occur.[1] Sometimes we lose the path, sometimes trip over a stone, sometimes fall headlong in the mud. We are beset by invitations to stray; by the attractive short cuts suggested by vanity, egoism or fear. We stand in perpetual need of the kindness and patience of that God who is our Guide no less than our Goal, who picks us up, overlooks our frailties and follies, again and again puts us back on the path. 'Forgive us our trespasses.' A whole type of prayer, a special and intimate relation with the Unseen, brought into existence by the very fact of our mixed half-animal nature, the ceaseless tension between the pull of earth

[1] *Pensées Diverses.* p. 111.

and the demand of heaven, is summed up in these four words.

Over against the Glory of God, the Majesty of the Holy, the debtor, the penitent, the publican, the unsatisfactory and unharmonized creature who exists in each of us dares to claim his filial rights. Here stands one who constantly falls short and knows it; who is blinded by prejudice, sick of self-love, capable of hatred and envy, violence and fear; one who could have done more and did not, thought he was strong and turned out weak, should not have trespassed in pursuits of his own ends, and did: a child of God, not an outsider or an outcast, who now faces the facts and says, 'Forgive!' Here, in the constant exercise of the divine economy of penitence and pardon, is one of the strongest links which binds the soul to God.

It is this desperate situation, whether corporate or individual, which we entreat God to accept and resolve: and this He can only do in one way—by making the utmost demand on the charity and humility of the creature, by a universal application of the law of generous love. Forgive us our trespasses, as we forgive them that trespass against us. We ask with confidence because we are the children of Love and have accepted its obligations, even though our own worst declensions will always be from Love itself, and our heaviest debts will be arrears of Charity. Yet here too, acknowledging our insufficiency, we are forgiven, if we try to look through the eyes of the divine pity on the failures of our brothers and sisters in love: forgetting our own injuries, however grevious, and remembering only our common tendency to sin.

If the Christian penitent dares to ask that his many departures from the Christian norm, his impatience, gloom, self-occupation, unloving prejudices, reckless tongue, feverish desires, with all the damage they have caused to Christ's Body, are indeed to be set aside, because—in spite of all—he longs for God and Eternal Life; then he too must set aside and forgive all that the impatience, selfishness, bitter and foolish speech, sudden yieldings to base impulse in others have caused him to endure. Hardness is the one impossible thing.

The Christian doctrine of forgiveness is so drastic and so difficult, where there is a real and deep injury to forgive, that only those living in the Spirit, in union with the Cross, can dare to base their claim on it. It means not only asking to be admitted to the Kingdom of Redeeming Love, but also declaring our willingness to behave as citizens of that Kingdom even under the most difficult conditions; the patriot king forgiving the invaders of his country, the merciful knight forgiving his brother's murderer and sheathing his sword before the crucifix, the parent forgiving his daughter's betrayer, the devoted reformer forgiving those who have ruined his life's work, the lover of peace forgiving the maker of war. Cruelty, malice, deceit and violence doing their worst; and seen by us through the eyes of a pitiful God. All this is supernatural, and reminds us again that the Lord's Prayer is a supernatural prayer: the prayer of the re-born, the realistic Christian who exists to do God's Will. Even so this clause comes a long way down: after the life of worship, the life of consecration, the prayer that the soul may be fed by the hand of God. Only then is it ready for this supreme test; this quiet and genial acceptance of the wounds of life, all the deliberate injury and the casual damage that come from lack of love; this prayer from the Cross. 'Love your enemies, and pray for them that persecute you.'

DELIVERANCE FROM EVIL

'Lead us not into temptation, but deliver us from evil.' May that strange directive power of which from time to time we are conscious as the controlling factor of life, have pity on our weakness and lead us out of confusion into peace.

This abject confession of helplessness seems

at first sight to be meant for the untried and
bewildered neophyte, in whom the gifts of
the Spirit have not yet had time to grow.
Actually, it is the culmination of the prayer
which was given to the Church of God in the
persons of her Apostles; those through whom
the sanctification of human history was to be
set going, the handful of men to whom we
owe our Christian inheritance. It is this
picked band, these channels of the Spirit,
already surrendered to the Creative Will,
who, as the very crown of filial worship, are
taught to acknowledge their own fragility,
their childlike status; their utter dependence
on the ceaseless guiding and protecting power
of God. 'My times are in Thy hand. . . . Hold
Thou up my going in Thy path that my footsteps slip not. . . .' All my small movements,
tests, struggles and apparent choices take
place within the grasp of Creative Love.
'Thou shalt answer for me, O Lord my God.'

We are committed to the life of the senses
with all its risks and deceits; and we know

well our own weakness, our inclination to sin. Yet we know too that in this confusion the rescuing power of the Holy is already active, and that if we are supple to His pressure we shall be kept from the temptations and delivered from the evil of a world in which grace and nature struggle together; in which the spirit of man, in spite of confusions and bewilderments, is never left alone.

It is from our own evil tendencies above all, our inveterate egotism with its million cunning disguises, our pride, greed and anger, our steadily downward drag to self-satisfaction that we need deliverance: for this we can never vanquish in our own strength. Do not let us be swamped in the strange tumult and conflict; the evil that results from the clash of wills unharmonized with Thy will. Deliver us by keeping clear that single relation with Thee which is our peace. We want the firm resistance of the over-ruling Spirit always present in the soul's deeps to the sudden up-rushes from lower centres of consciousness, the personal devils lodging in the basement, the interior hurly-burly of desires and dislikes; so easily aroused, so hard to quell. Our amphibious state is so delicately poised, so perilous, that only help from the higher can save us from being conquered by the lower. Deliver us from our share in the world's sin, our twist away from Holiness; reinforcing by your energetic grace our feeble will towards the good. We have reached now a vivid consciousness of 'that deep abyss of perversity' of which de Caussade speaks, into which, with so many others, we should fall if God did not hold us. 'It is only through their practical experience that the Saints have acquired that fundamental humility, that utter contempt and holy hatred of themselves of which we see so many proofs in the perfection.'[1] With them we ask that our divergent lives may be brought into line with that one Life in which evil did not operate;

[1] De Caussade. *Abandon à la Providence Divine*. Vol. 1, p. 229.

which escaped the doom laid upon this planet, and even in the extremity of suffering never faltered in its perfect response to the Father's Will.

'Lead us not into temptation.' Temptation is that sphere in which the evil dispositions which are present in the world—its whole trend towards self-satisfaction, self-fulfilment, and away from God—appear in their attractiveness and dominate the situation. We are not to presume on our strength and deliberately seek contact with that. This spoils the perfection of our meek abandonment to the Spirit; the subordination of our restless will to the steady pressure of God. To live by faith is to pursue quietly and in peace the path on which we are set, in the midst of the conflicts and confusions of the creature. In that quiet subordination is fulness of life; not in the passion for self-expression which tries every situation and every relationship and confuses pride with courage and initiative.

So austere, so arduous is the Christian programme, so real the struggle and so rough the journey to which the soul is called, that only when guided by a Spirit who knows the route better than we do, can we hope to get through without disaster. Any self-willed addition to life's difficulties brings its own punishment. There will be plenty of opportunity for courage, staying power and initiative as well as for humble obedience, for those who follow the guide's footsteps and are docile to His direction; some narrow ledges and treacherous slopes before we finish. All will be well if we do not yield to the temptation to tackle them alone; but there is every reason to fear the attractive short cut, the opportunity to satisfy our thirst for private spiritual adventure. The saints were driven on by rough tracks and awful darkness, in suffering and loneliness, by cloud and storm. They reached the summits; but never in their own strength or by following their own ideas—often indeed by taking what seems to onlookers the most unlikely route, because their feet were set upon a supernatural path which others cannot see.

What a deep and beautiful confidence it means if we are to accept this truth; not as a religious notion, but as the most massive fact of our strange mixed life, the culmination of our prayer. The ultimate humble trust of the little creature which first dared to say Abba, Father, is placed in the Absolute Love; and finds in the simple return to God the Unchanging, that personal and permanent relation which is the ground of prayer, the sovereign remedy against temptation, and defence against the assaults of the world's ill.

THE POWER AND THE GLORY

Thine is the Kingdom, the Power, and the Glory. The prayer in which is contained the whole movement of man's interior life, the substance of his communion with God, is summed up in this delighted declaration of the independent perfection, the unspeakable transcendence of the Holy. Before that reality, that majesty, that energy, that splendour, his own needs, his own significance vanish. Abba, Father. It is true that the Infinite God is the Father of my soul, that I have a certain kinship with the Abiding, a privilege of co-operation. Higher than my highest. He is yet nearer than my inmost part. But in the last resort, I stand entranced and abased before the majesty, the otherness of that Infinite God.

'He calleth the stars by their names.' All things, all mysteries, are brought to Him as their test and meaning. Thine is the Kingdom, hidden from our sight yet already present in perfection; Thy secret rule working from within, Thy secret pattern imposed on our chaos, Thy Spirit brooding on the deep, turning all things to Thy purpose, and even through conflicts, sin and anguish conditioning and transforming every aspect of human life. Thine is the Power, the inexaustible energy streaming forth from Thy hidden Being, by which the universe visible and invisible is

sustained. Thine is the Glory, the self-re-
vealed splendour of the Eternal Perfect filling
and transcending creation; seen in its hum-
blest beauties, yet never fully known. We
look beyond the ramparts of the world to that
triune Reality, the goal of our faith, hope and
love.

Yet even this Kingdom, Power and Glory,
this threefold manifestation of the character
of God, is not ultimate. The appeal of man's
prayer is to a Reality which is beyond manifestation. All these are Thine; but we reach
out to Thee. Beyond the wall of contradic-
tion, beyond the 'Light that is not God,' almost imperceptible to the attentive creature
and yet the ground of its being and goal of its
prayer, is the secret Presence; the Thou in
whom all things inhere, by whom all live.
Behind every closed door which seems to shut
experience from us He is standing; and within
every experience which reaches us, however
disconcerting, His unchanging presence is
concealed. Not in the wind which sweeps

over the face of existence to change it, not in
the earthquake which makes sudden havoc of
our ordered life, not in the overwhelming
splendour and fury of the elemental fire: in
none of these, but in the 'voice of gentle still-
ness,' speaking from within the agony and
bewilderment of life, we recognize the presence of the Holy and the completing answer
to the soul's completed prayer. We accept
Thy Majesty, we rejoice in Thy Power and
Thy Glory; but in Thine unchanging quiet is
our trust. We look beyond the spiritual to
Spirit, beyond the soul's country to the personal Origin and Father of its life.

'This is our Lord's will,' says Julian of Nor-
wich, 'that our prayer and our trust be both
alike large.' Step by step we have ascended
the hill of the Lord; and here at the summit
of our beseeching, conscious of our own lit-
tleness and the surrounding mystery, we
reach out in confidence to the All. The last
phase of prayer carries the soul forward to an
entire self-oblivion, an upward and outward

glance of awe-struck worship which is yet
entinctured with an utter and childlike trust.
Abba, Father. Thine is the kingdom, the
power and the glory. Thou art the Beginning
and the End of the soul's life.